T0198923

# QUALITY TEACHING

*Beating the Odds for At-Risk Students*

## VIOLA L. GRAYS-WILEY

WESTBOW
P R E S S®
A DIVISION OF THOMAS NELSON
& ZONDERVAN

WestBow Press books may be ordered through booksellers or by contacting:

WestBow Press
A Division of Thomas Nelson & Zondervan
1663 Liberty Drive
Bloomington, IN 47403
www.westbowpress.com
1 (866) 928-1240

ISBN: 978-1-9736-8343-8 (sc)
ISBN: 978-1-9736-8342-1 (e)

Print information available on the last page.

WestBow Press rev. date: 01/17/2020

This book is dedicated

To **my first teacher,**

My Mother,

**The late Fannie Mae Grays.**

It is further dedicated to the many

Parents across America who seek to

Make sense of the struggling

Public school systems,

Their mission and their

Vision for our youths.

# CONTENTS

# Acknowledgments

A fellow educator and close friend of mine told me that I should be getting the word out to all beginning teachers, as well as veteran teachers, about what it takes to be an effective teacher. She further stated that since I had actually had twenty-five years of teaching success, it would be a good idea to work at some of the neighboring universities in teacher training programs.

She said to me after a professional development presentation at the Illinois Institute of Technology, "Girl, you got it". Her face lit up as if I had just won the Olympic Gold Medal for Teaching, if there is such an award. Whatever, the "it" I had, she was extremely satisfied with my presentation. She was the individual in charge of getting professional consultants to present to beginning teachers at a Summer Fellows Workshop in the city of Chicago. I continued with my educational agenda of acquiring a Master's in Administration and Supervision with a Type 75 endorsement at Chicago State University. To me, this was the "it" that I wanted at that time. However, I continued presenting workshops and in-services to teachers within the city of Chicago and surrounding suburbs. With the number of positive evaluations I received, I started thinking, maybe I should seek to impact education on a larger scale by presenting to larger audiences of educators. Then I remembered being selected by my school's principal to present at the International Association of Behavioral Analysis Convention in downtown Chicago at the Hyatt-Regency. I was one of the keynote speakers. My mentor introduced me as "The Teacher's Teacher". His name was the late Dr. Ogden Lindsley. We all called him "Og". He is known as the "Father of Precision Teaching". Dr. Lindsley taught me the phenomenal benefits of charting in the classroom to remove learning deficits, and the positive energy it generates within the students to be accountable while tracking their daily success. *Amazing!!!* I would like to acknowledge all the workshop and in-service participants in Holmes County, in Mississippi, and in the Midwestern United States, for encouraging and inspiring me to do what I do. I first must acknowledge the Creator of the Universe, because through Him, all things are possible. To my family- Tarri, Jay, Meech, Terry, Debteen, Vicky, Darlene, D.D., and Annie Ruth, thank you for your continued support and inspiration. I have to acknowledge my former students from Vaiden High School, McClain Middle and McClain High Schools in Lexington, MS, Hearst Elementary and Caldwell Academy in the Chicago Public School System, Country Club Hills- SD 160 and in Hazel Crest, IL –Barack Obama Learning Academy and Jesse White Learning Academy. *Believe! Achieve! It's Possible!* I only know that within me, I have always had a passion for helping students to achieve success on a daily basis. I felt then, as I feel now, that if I teach them well, they will achieve well. If I want to know whether they

# INTRODUCTION

My beginning year as a classroom teacher started almost as strange as an individual being put into a jungle in a faraway country and left to survive and make the best of it. I was an elementary education major, with minors in language arts, reading and social work. After graduating from Mississippi Valley State University in Itta Bena, Mississippi, I was hired as a high school reading teacher for Grades 9 – 12. I literally had students in class who were older than I was. I was only nineteen at the time. Immediately, I knew I had to have my act together! About 80% of the students were African Americans, while the rest were white students. Since I wasn't even given a teacher's manual, I was told that the students who came to my class would need extra help with reading skills, lots of remediation. In other words, in today's terminology, they would be labeled as the "at-risk" group. Since they weren't primary or middle school students, I knew the materials I presented to them had to be interesting and "user-friendly", if you know what I mean. Therefore, I knew if I focused on vocabulary, novels, current news items, newspapers, magazines with celebrities and their lives, I could possibly maintain connectivity and classroom order simultaneously. Guess what, it worked! The students' reading scores improved dramatically because they "unknowingly" read a lot. Their spoken and written vocabularies were enhanced by the terminology presented through a wide genre of reading materials and daily practices of literacy skills. This debut teaching experience caused me to always be prepared to take students to their highest level of achievement by any means necessary. This experience ultimately led me to write this book… **for those who cause students to be at-risk**. My ultimate goal is for this book to become a required reading assignment for those who wish to enter the teaching profession. It is these individuals who will change the course of America's future. Be the teacher who gives every child a chance at success every day.

# A Child's First Teacher

A critical element in the development of a child is the child's first sounds. It is truly remarkable when a child is born with the physical and mental capabilities to hear and mimic sounds. It is just as crucial for these sounds to be warm and compassionate. Consider the parable of the Chinese Bamboo tree. This tree requires fertile soil, nurturing, watering, and sunshine. However, for the first four years, you will see no signs of growth or productivity, only the ground where you planted. But keep the faith, keep hope alive, perseverance, patience, because in that fifth year, a miracle happens. This tree grows as tall as 80 feet in just six weeks. Many children are similar to this tree, maybe not 80 feet in height, but cognitively, socially, emotionally, and yes, physical growth as well. As a child develops, s/he uses her/his senses of hearing, seeing, and touching more and more each day. By the time, a child reaches preschool, s/he has heard a world of sounds. Now the process begins of taking these sounds and discriminating as to what they all mean. The sound and picture connections begin. A year later in kindergarten, the child is expected to master recognition of the twenty-six letters of the English alphabets and letter-sound relationships. This is quite a plight for the young brain, but educators feel that this will lead students to academic success in the future. There are arguments for and against this train of thought. Some would suggest that this is too much to cram into the head of a five-year-old. Others might say that in a global view, this information should be mastered long before the kindergarten year. So much for the two arguments. I feel that the individual(s) who will be providing the nurturing and parenting to the child is the key figure(s) in masterminding the child's future success.

# WHO SHOULD (SHOULD NOT) BE A TEACHER ?

Is it fair to say that "Not everyone is cut out to be a teacher"? I simply ask this question because when things go wrong in the classroom, as they often do, this expression is either verbalized or secretly uttered in the heart and soul of the parent, guardian, administrator, or colleague next door to the teacher. You know I am expressing the truth, so you might as well say, "You know, you're right!" That brings me to this analytical self-survey that you should complete if you're thinking about, dreaming of, aspiring to become a TEACHER. Do a reality check by asking yourself these down-to-earth questions:

- Do I love children?

- Do I have or wish to have (adopt) children some day?

- If I have a child (or children), who will I trust to provide guidance and instruction to my child(ren)?

- Am I that kind of person?

- Do people often ask me to explain what I mean by statements I make?

- In my community, do I want children pointing me out to their parents?

- Do I display a respectable image within my family?

- After 3 – 5 years, do I plan to move to some other career choice?

If you answered yes to the first two questions, there is a 50% chance that you should consider teaching. The third and fourth questions are really pivotal ones. The questions are really asking if you have the qualities that parents and guardians look for in a teacher. Are **you** the kind of person that you would want instructing your child? The next question is a question of your didactical skills. How clear or explicit are you in getting a point across to a peer, family member, spouse, significant other, or any one? If you have problems expressing your point of view, it's almost a sure thing you will confuse many young minds as their instructional leader, along the way. Looking at the last two questions, we should realize that teaching is never concealed within the four walls of a classroom. Therefore, in the community, at the mall, at restaurants, and many other family-oriented venues, you may encounter your students in the presence of their parents/guardians. If this is not something you can handle, then maybe teaching is not for you. Remember, this is a reality check. There is hardly any place I can go to where I don't see former students who want to speak to me, introduce me to a parent, grandparent, foster parent, spouse, girlfriend, boyfriend, significant other, etc. Therefore, as teachers, we should know beforehand that our lives should be respectful ones. If you don't think this is a true possibility for you, then do the community  a favor and select another profession/

career choice. However, I must say there are some super teachers in every school building where I have worked. Many schools could improve from within through honor, collaboration and respect for teachers. *Without teachers, there are no other professions!*

(FOR THE COLLEGES & UNIVERSITIES)

# Teacher Preparation Programs

How effective are TEACHER PREPARATION PROGRAMS when it comes to dealing with the true populations of students who are entering classrooms today? Most of the research done has been on generations of students who followed the rules and routines of obtaining a quality education. How much research has been done or is being done on parents who have abused drugs and conceived children during the abuse of drugs? How much research has been done on parents who have eaten microwave food or fast food their entire lives and breakfast has always been a bag of chips? Teacher Preparation Programs, as we know them today, inadequately prepare new teachers for the real picture.

There are parents who were given a newborn to take home from the hospital without any parenting skills. Yes, this should change! New parents who have been "remote-controlled" from birth, or "microwaved" through life can offer very little parental involvement when it comes to assisting teachers with their child(children) educational framework. This is what $21^{st}$. century Teacher Preparation Programs should be addressing. Are the Teacher Preparation Programs in touch with true issues that prospective teacher candidates face on a daily basis? Considering all the texting, facebooking, twittering, tweeting, instagramming and incorporating these means of communication will be a challenge, but MUST BE addressed. Lecturing to an audience of teacher candidates should become more student-friendly/interactive through real-world situations by institutionalizing a global vision. We are truly in this together. When teachers fail, the world fails.

My journey as an undergrad student did very little to prepare me for the students I encountered during my early years as a teacher. In fact, I learned more in one week from the students in front of me than from the professors I had for four years. This is what I mean by "Teacher Preparation Programs" being out of touch with reality. Teacher Preparation Programs should include regular visits to schools to observe the best and the brightest, the middle-of-the-road (mediocre) students, the lowest level of regular education students, as well as the many special needs classrooms that exist. Following each visit, in-depth dialogue should occur. Questions like…

- What happened?
- What would you do differently?
- How effective was that teacher with_____?
- What part of School Law was involved in that particular event?
- Were there any Special Education issues involved?
- What does the research say about similar scenarios?

This would make teaching real. Teacher Preparation Programs should be practical. This type of preparedness would increase teacher retention rates. There is no better feeling than going to a new job when you are totally prepared for each obstacle set before you. You have a feeling of confidence that can never be mistaken. This helps you to feel the positive energy that you need to be successful.

# Systems Designed to Fail Students

You know in a Utopia, no school system would be designed to fail students. However in school systems across the United States of America, I beg the differ. If your school system is not designed for students to experience optimal success on a daily basis, then it is designed for students to experience failure or defeat. Students, like adults, want to be successful. They want to feel good about themselves. I would like for independent groups to travel across America and walk into the schools where every single student has a laptop computer and travel a few miles up or down the road or street, and there may only be only one classroom in the building that has Internet access. To the tons of philanthropists in this country, the Land of the Free and the Home of the Brave, I challenge you to physically visit schools across America and then put your money where the needs are. I would even challenge you to go further: make a return visit to see if things are better because of you. If they are, then you have truly made a difference in the lives of America's children and your living has not been in vain. There are too many billionaires and millionaires in this country for our students to be so deprived of bare educational essentials: a house, food, clothing, books, a computer, a calculator. Just bare essentials…

Instead, there are figures in this country who want to invest and finance more and more correctional facilities: PRISONS. Maybe you should just think…What if we educated the students at equivocal levels where they could compete globally with peers from any country, then wouldn't it be interesting to see how crime rates dwindle? Wouldn't it be nice to go outside and greet the neighbor next door and exchange a few words about the stock market quotes in yesterday's newspaper because the neighbor was highly intelligent like yourself? The neighbors could all read and interpret data in graphs and tables. Wouldn't this just be the edge that America needed to regain its strength in a global economy! Somewhere in the back of your mind, you'll hear me saying, "I told you so!"

The educational system in America should focus on diminishing its financial support for the penal systems and replenishing its resources for schools and instructional endeavors. Schools are the "grass-root" institutions that can impact the quality of life for all in a country.

We should re-design schools for success. Teach students what ever they need to be successful. If job applications require bilingualism, then teach a second language to all students. If there are language barriers, remove them. Educate students while promoting success for the entire community. We are truly in this together. When schools succeed, America succeeds.

# At-Risk Students' Plight

Students who are at-risk of being successful in life, realize this by the time they are in first grade. These students are soon labeled by the educated world as "At-Risk". They have received this label either because they have a unique style of learning or because the teacher was part of a poor teacher preparation program and failed to bond with the students. I know this might sound cruel to you, especially coming from a teacher with twenty-five years of successful teaching under her belt. But this is the very reason I can say these words with absolute affirmation. I truly feel that many of my former teachers should have been labeled "At-Risk". I even feel that some teachers that I have visited for my son's Parent-Teacher Conferences should have been similarly labeled as well.

Why should a teacher give a student 50 or more words to define as part of one homework assignment? If a child actually masters 5 – 10 new words per subject per day, this child is truly going to have a successful and educated life. Why 50 words per subject? Wouldn't you agree that this teacher is "At-Risk" of devastating the lives of many children unless she retires and seeks a new career now? Teaching is not for him (her). Therefore, students who do not master skills the first time they are taught, should simply be taught the skill using different strategies. I was always bored with a teacher when I had to sit in a hard seat more than 30 minutes. I needed to move something! There are many students becoming "At-Risk" because they are bored to death!!! Teachers, if you absorb nothing else from reading this book, MASTER this…MAKE LEARNING FUN!!! Engage all students in meaningful learning experiences. If you believe, they will achieve.

# GETTING TO KNOW STUDENTS

You know this seems so simple, but it's the one little **key element** that is often missing in classrooms where there are management problems. Students will move mountains for teachers who go the extra mile to get to know them. It can be something so minute as remembering their birthdays with a pencil and a picture of their favorite pets. Little things still mean a lot!

Those first weeks of school should be weeks of teacher-student bonding. Wow! It does so much for the rest of the school year. It alleviates at least 90% of the discipline problems you would have incurred. You wonder about the value of years of teaching experience? Well, this is what it yields: KNOWLEDGE and EXPERTISE. Nothing beats experience.

No matter what your schedule says, your administrator will appreciate the fact that you **can teach** because of your excellent classroom management skills. It is an absolute "MUST" that you gain control of your class before you attempt to disperse knowledge. You can start with… "The scariest movie I ever saw was this move about a monster with three legs and five eyes. I was so scared that I told my momma' I was going to sleep with her until I graduated from high school. I was only in second grade then. Has anyone else ever seen a scary movie or anything like that?" What really matters is that you start bonding. You can talk about going to a country place or traveling over the long Mississippi River Bridge or even eating deer sausages for breakfast. This was always a real treat for me in Black Hawk, Mississippi! My brothers, Terry, D.D., and Chris, love to hunt for deer. My sister Darlene always has the skillet ready for the sausages. I love country eating!" What I am trying to say is… Just start a bonding dialogue. They have a lot they want to share with an audience, led by a person *(teacher)*, who truly cares. Get to know your students so that when something goes a little to the left, you can pull that student aside and say something like… "Tamika, you really let me down when you_____. I want to count on you as a team leader in my class, so

_____". Bonding really helps. You will never know all of the behavioral situations you averted by using those beginning weeks of the school year to get students to "buy in" to a set of rules that they come up with, along with consequences and rewards. They will let their classmates know which rule is being broken and the consequences that will possibly follow, if this peer doesn't get his/her act together. The fact that these rules will assist in them becoming active learners each day, no one gets the opportunity to fall behind or become "at-risk" due to misbehaviors. Many students labeled as "at-risk" have wonderful leadership skills that haven't been cultivated. As educators, we have to learn to accentuate the positives every single day that we step into a classroom because by the time some students get to school in the morning, they have been "put down" at least a dozen times. Sometimes this happens in the home, other times, it may occur on their way to school, on the bus, down the street, and in high crime areas, the journey to school has been so challenging that only a friend who's been down that road, would truly understand. So when students show up for school, welcome them with knowledge, care, concern, and daily supports. "I'm having a great day because you are here!"

# TEACHABLE OPPORTUNITIES

Every moment in school should be viewed by educators as teachable opportunities. When students enter the school building in the morning and head down the hall for breakfast, if there is something you can say or do to impact student learning or student behavior, don't delay, DO IT! SAY IT! When I look at how fast the world is changing and the fact that new things are being added every day, as if the old things have already been acquired, I want to put so much knowledge into the head of each student I encounter every single day. In fact, the day is never long enough! I know some teachers are reading this and thinking, "What is she on?" But the truth of the matter is, you will not encounter a student that I have taught within the last 25 years who will say any thing differently. I used every teachable opportunity as a learning experience. When my eight grade students on the West Side of Chicago entered the classroom, they entered with a ticket. This ticket was usually an essay they had written the night before on some interesting topic. I allowed the students to select relevant topics. These topics reflected what was going on in the world around them: drug abuse by relatives, teenage pregnancy, abortions, recruitment by gang members, babysitting siblings, etc. As a result, these students were learning the elements of the writing process without thinking about it as homework. The essays had to be focused on the topic, coherent, grammatically checked and signed by a peer for convention errors, and then submitted to me. They were meeting after school any way. I simply gave them a more defined purpose. They could share with the class if they desired to. Most wanted to share their writing pieces. This was an enjoyable, interactive learning experience for them.

I never had to ask for order. They were quiet so they could hear these essays. Each student would ask at the end, "How could I make my essay even better?" The class would give them different wording or simply say, "That was a good essay!" They weren't allowed to use the real names of relatives.

My fifth graders at S. V. Marshall Elementary School in Tchula, Mississippi, were some of the best writers the Superintendent of the Holmes County School District had ever seen. He was so impressed with their writing that I was pulled out of the classroom to present writing in-services to teachers in the entire school district (K-12). As a teacher, you should give it your best every single day.

# Global Visions for Students

I don't think any person or organization can succeed without having a defined vision. Most schools have a Mission and Vision Statement. Sometimes they are combined; sometimes they are separate. However, schools realize that they need to have a vision in order to set goals to achieve. I feel that each teacher should post his (her) vision for his(her) students and read daily until it is mentally and physically a part of his(her) daily actions. How can you determine your vision for your students? Here are some questions to guide your thought process:

- What do I want my students to know by the end of the day?

- What should my students be expected to perform by the end of the day?
- How will I know they are learning?
- What will I do if they are not learning?
- Where will my students score nationally as a result of my teaching?
- How will life be better in the world because of what I have taught my students?
- Am I preparing my students for colleges/careers?

Answers to these questions should formulate a vision for teachers around the world, not just in America. Better yet, why not let America be the example for others to follow?

# EXPECTATIONS FOR SUCCESS

At the beginning of each school year, students should receive a list of supplies needed, books, class schedules, and above all, expectations for the school year. Before the students receive any of this, the teachers should have already established their expectations for a successful school year. Let me clarify what I really mean here. I am not referring to a year with a minimal number of office referrals. What I am really referring to is students mastering essential skills due to teachers' strategic lesson planning within a fun-filled learning environment. With this in mind, I feel that students will encounter successful learning experiences on a daily basis. I've often heard the expression that you can eat an elephant if he's cut into small enough pieces. I guess what this really means is that if we (the teachers) break learning down to the students' instructional level and provide challenges for them, they will rise to meet our levels of expectation through the provision of adequate instructional support (intervention, remediation, or enrichment).

Teachers should say to students: At the end of this lesson, I expect you to know_____and be able to _____ because this will help you _____.

Don't make students wonder what you want them to know and why they need to know it. TELL them!!! Remove the option of guessing. **Let each student expect and experience success every day!!!**

# Thoughts to Ponder...

Do you sleep so much better at night because you have failed half of your class or more? Do you wish more of your students could master the skills you are teaching them? Whatever your answer to these questions are, only you will ever know how you really feel about the knowledge you are entrusted to impart to the students in your classroom. Know this: In today's society, the life you save could be your own. If I receive the wrong medication, it could be linked to the fact that I provided poor education to the student who is now filling my prescription.

Give education your all. A good friend of my family, Mr. L. Susberry, always stressed to us that the fence that separates poverty from prosperity is education. I guess this was the plight of Crispus Attucks, Sojourner Truth, Benjamin Banneker, Carter G. Woodson, Harriet Tubman, Eleanor Roosevelt, Thurgood Marhsall, Brown vs. Board of Education, Dr. Martin Luther King, Jr., and many more before and since then. Now, it remains the struggle of my parents, your parents, and the teachers who are still within this global quest each and every day.

# A CHANCE

## THE PERFECT Must Read for...

Parents/Guardians

Teachers (All Disciplines)

School Administrators

Assistant Teachers

School Board Members

College Professors

Students Majoring in Education

State Board Educators

Education Stakeholders

Printed in the United States
By Bookmasters